641.5

The
WILD, WILD
COOKBOOK

ALSO BY JEAN C. GEORGE:

Moon of the Moles
Cry of the Crow
The Grizzly Bear with the Golden Ears
Going to the Sun
Julie of the Wolves
Wounded Wolf

The
WILD, WILD
COOKBOOK

A GUIDE FOR YOUNG WILD-FOOD FORAGERS

by Jean Craighead George

ILLUSTRATED BY WALTER KESSELL

Thomas Y. Crowell   *New York*

Library of Congress Cataloging in Publication Data
George, Jean Craighead, 1919–
    The wild, wild cookbook.
    Includes index.
    Summary: A field guide for finding,
harvesting, and cooking wild plants,
arranged by season.
    1. Cookery (Wild foods)—Juvenile literature.
    2. Wild plants, Edible—Juvenile literature.
    [1. Wild plants, Edible. 2. Cookery—Wild
foods] I. Kessell, Walter, ill. II. Title.
TX823.G45 1982   641.5'78   82–45187
ISBN 0–690–04314–7   AACR2
ISBN 0–690–04315–5 (lib. bdg.)
ISBN 0–690–04319–8 (pbk.)
1 2 3 4 5 6 7 8 9 10
First Edition

CONTENTS

You should not use this book by yourself until you have learned how to identify wild plants from a specialist or someone knowledgeable in this area.

The
WILD, WILD
COOKBOOK

INTRODUCTION

When the flicker returns to my lawn in spring and the flowers of the shadbush shine like frost in the dark woodland, I am reminded that it is time to whip up a batch of Dandelion Fritters or a Fiddlehead Pie. It is April, and another foraging season has begun.

A penknife, a bag, and fingers are the tools of the craft. The wild crops are found along roadsides and waterways, in fields, forests, city parks, vacant lots, and even on city sidewalks where acorns fall and purslane pushes up through cracks in the cement.

I am the third of four generations of wild-food gatherers who take to the hills and fields in spring, summer, and autumn to harvest the free-growing plants, cook, and eat them. Grandfather taught my father, my father taught me, and I taught my children where the violets bloom and the lamb's-quarters flourish.

We do not necessarily wander far from our doors. My daughter who now lives in the city finds chicory and plantain in parks and abandoned lots. I pick tasty weeds along roadsides or in fields and marshes near my suburban home. My own lawn is a weed feast. The grass-lands and desert of my youngest son's south-west home offers a variety of pot herbs for his table.

And there is the serendipity—the unsought gifts of foraging: learning the names and fami-lies of plants and the birds and beasts they sup-port. As a bonus we discover wondrous habitats: cool waterfalls, fern-luminous groves. Sometimes we are diverted by an ant collecting aphids for her tribe or a Baltimore oriole pull-ing threads from a grapevine to weave into a basket nest. Most important, we see the inter-dependency of plant, bird, beast, and human. We understand why we must protect our van-ishing wilderness and farmlands. And we have joined conservation societies to fight for them. Once you have learned from a knowledgeable person how to identify wild plants, you can use this book to increase the knowledge that you already have. When in doubt do not taste a plant. Knowing your plants is the best insur-ance against accidental poisoning. Make sure that you know what you are gathering before you use any of the recipes in this book. If you are not sure about the identity of a plant take it to an expert such as a teacher or a naturalist at a nature center for identification before doing anything further. Most plants are safe, but certainly not all are safe, nutritious, or tasty.

Begin foraging by only picking a plant you know well. The dandelion is a good one since most people learned it with their ABC's; it is nationwide in distribution and a "weed." No one will stop you from picking dandelions. Violets, cacti, garlic, and oxalis are good follow-up plants once you know how to identify them; they can be learned at a glance and all but violets are unloved.

Mushrooms I pass by. They are difficult to identify and so dangerous that a professor of mycology once told me that he himself would never pick and eat wild mushrooms, expert as he was. "They are too confusing," he said, "even when examined under a microscope." So I, too, leave them alone.

Of the more than 25,000 plant species in North America, only a few are poisonous; most of these are mushrooms. The others should be learned. Poison ivy and oak and deadly nightshade are the most often encountered; I have yet to find poison sumac in all my wanderings outdoors. Poison hemlock resembles Queen Anne's lace and grows in dry ground the country across. Its hollow, grooved stems are spotted with purple, the telltale clue to its identity. The juices are very poisonous.

This book is divided into seasonal foraging sections: spring, summer, autumn, and all year 'round. Plants are illustrated and their descriptions and habitats given. The plants in each section are listed alphabetically. Recipes follow the identification section. In our family the cooking as well as the foraging is shared by everyone: boys, men, girls, women. Preparing wild foods is a time of camaraderie.

The recipes are written for the modern kitchen, but many can be made over a campfire or in a rock oven, a method that tenderizes and flavors not only wild plants but game and fish as well.

ROCK OVEN

1. Dig a saucer-shaped hole in the ground about three feet across and a foot and a half deep. Line it with hand-sized rocks. Keep the dirt.
2. Build a fire in the rock saucer and let it burn until the rocks are hot and sizzle when water is dropped on them.
3. Remove the logs and embers with a shovel, and either douse them or add wood to make a campfire.

4. Line the pit with a bed of green grass or moistened leaves such as arrowhead or corn husks.
5. Wrap plants, fish, or game in aluminum foil or leaves, after seasoning with salt, pepper, and herbs. Breads and pies should be placed in lidded pots with room for them to rise.
6. Place foods on the grass bed.
7. Cover with grass, corn husks, or leaves.
8. Cover with damp cloth, dish towels, or burlap bag.
9. Shovel the dirt over the cloth.
10. In about two hours the meal is ready to eat. My twenty-one-pound Thanksgiving turkey cooked in three hours.

THE FEAST

Our family serves wild foods on linen tablecloths with the best china and silver. In the back country we dine around a campfire or sit before an inspiring view of forest, prairie, or mountain. No matter where we are, the banquet table is permeated with a sense of achievement and freedom. I know of no other pursuit with such rewards.

SPRING

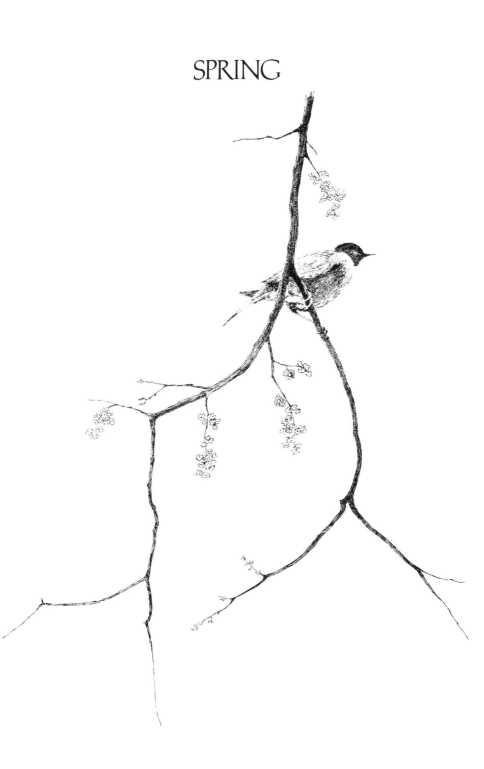

BRACKEN FERN

SCIENTIFIC NAME: *Pteridium aquilinum*

APRIL–MAY

Ferns grow everywhere except the arid deserts. Although some are abundant, there are not many species, perhaps 200 in North America. Fortunately, the common ones are profuse and easily identified: the Christmas fern with its dark green leaflets shaped like a child's boot, the cinnamon fern with its tall leaves and brownish hairy stems. The bracken fern and the small common polypody are also easy to know. In the spring of the year all ferns send up fiddleheads, leaves that unfurl like coiled clock springs. All are good to eat, but some are not worth the effort of cleaning the fuzz from them, like the furry cinnamon fern. Since the bracken fern is widely spread over North America, and for that matter the world, and since it is easy to identify, delicious, and often considered a weed, I'll discuss it.

The commonest of our ferns, the bracken or brake fern, is strong and coarse. It continues to produce new leaves all season. The mature, almost horizontal leaves are dark green, three feet long and three feet wide, and usually divided into three nearly equal parts.

The fiddleheads look like an eagle's claw and are covered with silvery gray hairs that can be removed by brushing or running the fingers along them. The coils should be picked when five or six inches tall and tender. Boil the fiddleheads twice to insure sweetness.

The bracken fern grows in the full sun, in woods, old pastures, along dry roadsides and in burned-over areas and thickets. It prefers poor soils rather than the rich limy soils sought by most ferns.

FRIED FIDDLEHEADS

April–May

Ingredients
1 cup bracken fern or other fiddleheads
2 pots of boiling water
2 tablespoons butter

Utensils
3-quart saucepan
Colander
Frying pan
Large spoon

Directions
1. Place fern fiddleheads in boiling water.
2. Simmer for 15 minutes. Drain, set aside.
3. Bring water to a boil once more.
4. Put fiddleheads in boiling water for 15 minutes.
5. Drain.
6. Melt butter in frying pan.
7. Sauté fiddleheads until brown and tender.
8. Serve hot.

FIDDLEHEAD PIE

(Also dandelions, watercress, faun lily bulbs, chicory, plantain, milkweed buds and pods)

Oven: 450° F, then 350° F.   Time: 10–20 minutes

Ingredients
  1 baked pie shell
  1 cup bracken or other fiddleheads
  4 Jerusalem artichokes (optional) or cattail rhizome (optional)
    Water
  2 tablespoons butter
  2 tablespoons flour
  ¾ cup milk
  2 chicken bouillon cubes
  ¼ cup water
  ½ cup grated cheese of your choice. (I like Vermont cheddar.)
  ¾ teaspoon salt
    Pepper
  ¼ cup Parmesan cheese
  3 hard-boiled eggs

Utensils
Pie plate
Colander
3-quart saucepan
Measuring spoon
Measuring cup
Mixing spoon
Cheese grater

Directions

1. Bake pie shell at 450°F for 5 minutes or until pale brown. Remove from oven.
2. Turn oven to 350°F.
3. Wash and drain fiddleheads and Jerusalem artichokes or cattail tubers, if used.
4. Cover with water and boil for 10 minutes.
5. Drain well. Boil again, and drain.
6. Melt butter slowly in saucepan.
7. Add flour and stir butter and flour until well mixed.
8. Slowly add milk. Keep stirring until sauce is thickened.
9. Dissolve bouillon cubes in ¼ cup hot water. Add to sauce.
10. Stir grated cheese into sauce.
11. Add salt and pepper.
12. Lightly stir in fiddleheads and Jerusalem artichokes.
13. Pour into baked pie shell.
14. Sprinkle Parmesan cheese over top.
15. Decorate with sliced hard-boiled eggs.
16. Bake in 350°F oven until cheese browns.
17. Cut into wedges and serve hot.

Fiddlehead Pie can be made a day ahead and kept in refrigerator before baking.

CATTAILS

SCIENTIFIC NAME: *Typha* (VARIOUS SPECIES)

APRIL–JUNE

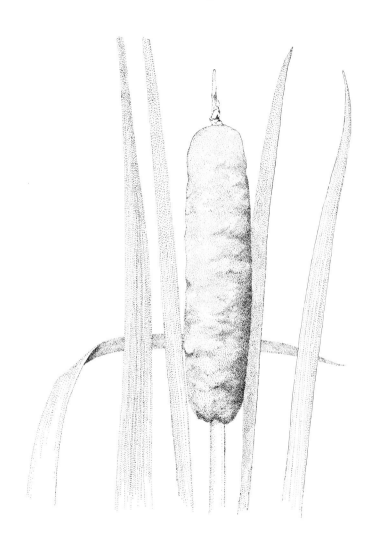

Cattails are tall, strap-leafed plants with hot-dog-shaped heads. They grow all over the United States in marshes, clustering together in dense colonies. Some species are waist high, others are twice as tall as a man. The four species in the United States are the Broadleaf, Narrowleaf, Southern, and Blue Cattail. All are distinguished in summer by stems topped with those brown seed heads, which can be from an inch to a foot and a half long depending on the species. The big ones are the Big Southern and Blue Cattails.

Early in the growing season, usually when the Azaleas are blooming, the leaf spikes are tender and edible. When they are about one or two feet tall, no bigger, they should be cut, washed, and peeled down to their whitish-green core. They can be eaten raw or cooked. The flower spikes, the cattails-on-the-cob, grow on distinctively narrow stems compared to the leaf spikes, and taste very much like corn. The pollen or male flower appears on the top of the spike like a golden "tail" about one inch above the female flowers. It is a powder and is used as a flour in breads, pancakes, and cakes. The underground part of the cattails, or rhizomes, are a nourishing starch. Dig with a shovel until you see the ropelike structures growing laterally. Pull up and cut off sections of the rhizome. Bake or boil.

INDIAN CATTAIL SPOON BREAD

Oven: 400° F   *Time: 10 minutes*

Ingredients	*Utensils*
½ cup butter	Chopping board
2 cups fresh flower buds	Knife
or cattails-on-the-cob,	Measuring cup
scraped from 4 to 5	9″ skillet
dozen uncooked cattail	Mixing spoon
bud spikes	9″ greased
½ cup diced onions	bread pan
½ green pepper, diced	
Salt	
1 cup sharp cheddar-	
type cheese, shredded	
Pinch of chili powder	

Directions
1. Melt butter in skillet.
2. Add cattail buds.
3. Add onions, pepper, and salt. Cook 5 minutes.
4. Pour into greased baking dish.
5. Sprinkle with cheese and dot with pinch of chili powder.
6. Bake until cheese melts.
7. Serve hot.

CATTAIL-ON-THE-COB

Ingredients   *Utensils*
Young cattail buds   12-quart pot

Directions
1. Remove sheaths from young cattail buds.
2. Plunge spikes into boiling water.
3. Boil rapidly for 15 minutes.
4. Butter and salt, and eat like corn-on-the-cob.

CATTAIL LEAF SPIKES

Ingredients   *Utensils*
Young cattail leaf spikes,   12-quart pot
gathered before the
plant is more than 2
feet high

Directions
1. Scrub spikes.
2. Peel and uncover the crisp whitish-green core, usually 1 foot to 18 inches long.
3. Slice core raw into salads,
   or
4. Boil in salt water about 15 minutes.
5. Serve as a vegetable, with butter and salt.

CAT-O-NINE-TAIL PANCAKES

Cattail pollen, which is sacred to the Apaches, is quite easy to collect. When the pollen forms on the top of the flower stalk, bend the heads into a plastic or paper bag and shake the pollen into it. A dozen plants will yield about a cup. Wear boots or old sneakers, because your feet will get muddy and wet—it's worth it.

Ingredients
- 1 cup cattail pollen
- 1 cup white flour
- 2½ teaspoons baking soda
- ¾ teaspoon salt
- 1 egg, well beaten
- 1¼ cups milk
- 3 tablespoons vegetable oil or butter
- Butter or oil for frying
- Maple syrup, wild jam, or jellies

Utensils
- Mixing bowl
- Measuring cup
- Measuring spoon
- Griddle or skillet
- Pancake turner

Directions
1. Mix cattail pollen, flour, soda, and salt.
2. Stir in egg, milk, and oil.
3. Set aside until batter thickens, about 10 minutes.

4. Bake on hot oiled griddle.
5. Serve with maple syrup or wild jellies and jams.

MUFFINS OF GOLD

Oven: 400°F   *Time: 20 minutes*

Ingredients

1 cup cattail pollen
1 cup whole wheat flour
2½ teaspoons baking powder
½ teaspoon salt
2 tablespoons sugar, or ⅓ cup honey
1 egg, well beaten
1 cup milk
¼ cup oil or melted butter

Utensils

2 mixing bowls
Mixing spoon
Measuring cup
Measuring spoons
Eggbeater
2 12-hole muffin pans, greased or lined with paper cups

Directions

1. Combine cattail pollen, flour, baking powder, salt, and sugar, if used.
2. Beat egg, add to it the milk, oil, and honey, if used.

3. Mix wet and dry ingredients, stirring quickly for about 10 seconds. Ignore the lumps.
4. Fill greased muffin pans.
5. Bake about 20 minutes.

CHOLLA

SCIENTIFIC NAMES: *Opuntia fulgide*

(MANY VARIETIES)

MARCH–MAY

The cholla, also known as the staghorn or jumping cactus, is a very spiny cactus with twiglike joints. The flowers are bright yellow, orange, red, or magenta. This distinctive plant is found in the desert up to 4,000 feet in southwestern Colorado, southwestern Utah, southern Nevada, southern California, western New Mexico, and western Arizona.

In March, before the flowers open in April and May, the buds should be picked and de-thorned. Fill two saucepans one-third full of washed gravel. Add the cholla buds, and pour from one pan to the other until the thorns are banged off. Five or six tosses are necessary. Check to make sure the thorns are gone. If not, rub off the remainder, wearing a pair of work gloves or by using tweezers. When all the buds have been de-thorned, wash under running cold water. These buds are very rich in calcium.

COOKED CHOLLA BUDS

Utensils
3-quart saucepan

Directions
1. Place de-thorned buds in saucepan.
2. Cover with water.
3. Boil for 15 minutes.
4. Drain.
5. Serve with butter and salt, or put in salad or meat stew, or add to cornmeal mush.

DANDELION

SCIENTIFIC NAME: *Taraxacum officinale*

APRIL–MAY (MOST ABUNDANT)

Everyone knows the dandelion, or will after one look. The leaves grow close to the ground and flare outwards from a central core. The bright yellow flowers are borne on single hollow stems and are made up of a hundred or more little flowers or florets.

The common dandelion grows all over the United States in open moist places, digging their long taproots down into lawns, pastures, gardens, and roadsides.

Dandelions can be spotted at a distance by that round silver blowball. The seeds or akenes are topped with plumes that travel like parachutes when the wind or kids blow them, sending them sailing to new homes. Gather the blowballs and put them in your bird feeder to attract goldfinches, pine siskins, yellowheaded blackbirds, and towhees.

The dandelion was brought from Europe to New England by the first immigrants and has now spread all over the West in grass seed and in bird droppings. One of the most versatile of the wild plants, this persistent species sustained many a homesteader and pioneer.

DANDELION FRITTERS

Ingredients
- 1 cup biscuit mix
- 1 cup milk
- 1 tablespoon sugar or honey (optional)
- ½ inch oil in skillet
- 4 cups dandelion flower heads, snapped off at top of stem

Utensils
- Skillet or deep fry pan
- Mixing bowl
- Measuring cup
- Measuring spoons
- Fry tongs or spoon
- Paper bag or toweling for draining
- For storing, coffee can with plastic lid

Directions
1. Mix together the biscuit mix, milk, and sugar or honey, if used.
2. Heat oil in skillet to 325–335°F or until it sizzles when a bit of batter is dropped into it.
3. Dip dandelion flowers in mix, one at a time, and douse well.
4. Drop flowers into hot oil, head first.
5. Fry until golden brown.
6. Turn with tongs or fry-spoon and brown other side.

7. Remove and place on brown paper bag or toweling to drain.
8. Repeat with the remaining flowers.
9. Eat hot or cold.
10. Store leftovers in coffee can and place in refrigerator for snacks.

DANDELION FRITTERS WITHOUT BISCUIT MIX

Ingredients
  2 eggs, well beaten
⅔ cup milk
  1 cup flour
  1 teaspoon baking
    powder
¼ teaspoon salt
    Pepper (optional)
½ inch oil in skillet
  4 cups dandelion flower
    heads, snapped off at
    top of stem

Utensils
Same as in recipe
  for Dandelion
  Fritters

Directions
1. Beat eggs.
2. Add milk.
3. Mix flour, baking powder, salt, and pepper, if used.
4. Slowly add dry ingredients to eggs and milk.
5. Heat oil in saucepan until batter sizzles.
6. Drop dandelions in batter, and fry until golden brown.

DANDELION CROWNS

1. Using a trowel, dig deep under the dandelion, lift up, and gently pull up root, leaves and all.
2. Wash well.
3. Cut off the roots and save for dandelion coffee.
4. In between the roots and the leaves lies the white crown. Cut off the leaves about ½ inch above the crown and save the leaves for dandelion salad.

Ingredients	*Utensils*
1 cup dandelion crowns	Sharp knife or
3 cups water	scissors
2 tablespoons butter	Measuring
½ teaspoon salt	spoons
Pepper	Measuring cup
	3-quart saucepan

Directions
1. Wash crowns to remove the last bit of grit.
2. Cover with 1½ cups water and boil 5 minutes.
3. Pour off water and repeat once more or until all bitterness is gone. I pour off only one water—I like the bitter snap.
4. Serve hot with butter, salt, and pepper.

TWO-FACED DANDELION SANDWICH

Ingredients
- 2 eggs, slightly beaten
- ½ cup water or milk
- 8 slices white, rye, wholewheat, or other bread
- 1 cup dandelion flowers (no stems)
- 4 tablespoons margarine or butter

Utensils
- Measuring cup
- Measuring spoons
- Griddle or skillet
- Pancake turner

Directions
1. Mix eggs and milk or water.
2. Dip 4 slices of bread into egg mix.
3. Place dandelion flowers on 4 dipped slices.
4. Dip and cover with other 4 slices.
5. Fry sandwiches in margarine or butter until golden brown on both sides. Fry slowly.

For variation: Add Mayapple fruits, sprinkled with a mixture of 2 tablespoons sugar and ½ teaspoon cinnamon.

Serve with maple syrup, honey, or wild jellies or jams.

Another variation: A slice of your favorite cheese on top of the dandelions.

BOILED DANDELION GREENS

Ingredients
4 cups dandelion leaves,
   washed well
½ teaspoon salt
 1 cup boiling water
 1 tablespoon butter
   Pepper

Utensils
Colander
3–quart saucepan
Measuring cup
Measuring
  spoons
Mixing spoon
Colander

Directions
1. Put dandelion leaves in saucepan. Add salt.
2. Heat water in tea kettle.
3. Pour ½ cup water over greens.
4. Simmer the dandelion leaves 5 minutes. Pour off the water.
5. Pour remaining boiling water over greens and simmer until tender, about 10 minutes.
6. Serve topped with butter and a dash of pepper and salt.

WILTED DANDELION GREENS

Ingredients
4 cups dandelion leaves
  (These can be picked

Utensils
Colander
Salad bowl

Ingredients (cont.)

all year around if the
tender center leaves
are chosen.)
4 strips bacon, diced and
cooked crisp
2 tablespoons sugar
Salt
Pepper
¼ teaspoon dry mustard
3 tablespoons cider
vinegar
2 hard-boiled eggs

Utensils (cont.)

Skillet
Measuring cup
Measuring
spoons
Fork
Sharp knife

Directions

1. Wash dandelion greens in colander, dry and place in salad bowl.
2. Fry bacon in pan until crisp.
3. Remove bacon and drain on paper. Save the bacon fat.
4. Add sugar, salt, pepper, dry mustard, and cider vinegar to bacon fat.
5. Heat until the sugar has dissolved.
6. Pour the mixture over the dandelion leaves.
7. Add crisp bacon, and toss well.
8. Slice hard-boiled eggs and garnish the salad with them.
9. Serve while hot.

DANDELION ROOT COFFEE

Spring, summer, fall   *Oven: 200°–300° F*

Directions

1. Scrub the roots with a stiff vegetable brush.
2. Scrape off as much of the tough outer skin and rootlets as possible.
3. Place roots on a cookie sheet and dry in a low oven until brown and brittle, about 2½ hours.
4. Grind the snappy dry roots in a coffee-bean grinder or food chopper.

DANDELION ROOT
COFFEE FOR TWO

Ingredients

2½ cups water in pot or
saucepan
2 heaping teaspoons
ground dandelion
roots
Cream
Sugar

Utensils

Saucepan or
cowboy coffee
pot
Teaspoon

Directions

1. Bring water to a boil.
2. Add dandelion coffee.
3. Boil 10 minutes.
4. Strain into cups.
5. Lace with cream and sugar and enjoy.

WEEDY LAWN SALAD

Ingredients

1 cup tender dandelion greens

¼ cup each of plantain leaves, violet leaves, chicory, purslane, oxalis (all of these grow in my lawn, hence the salad's name)

½ cup favorite cheese (Swiss), cut into strips

½ cup boiled ham, cut into strips

2 hard-boiled eggs, sliced

1 tablespoon wild garlic tops (optional)

3 tablespoons vegetable oil

1 tablespoon cider vinegar

½ teaspoon salt

Utensils

Colander
Salad bowl
Cutting board
Cutting knife
Measuring cup
Measuring spoon

Directions

1. Wash greens and pat dry.
2. Mix greens in salad bowl.

3. Add cheese and ham and sliced hard-boiled eggs.
4. Add garlic if you like it.
5. Add oil and toss.
6. Add vinegar and salt and toss.
7. Garnish with violets, forsythia, day-lily flowers, or rose petals.

LAMB'S-QUARTERS

SCIENTIFIC NAME: *Chenopodium album*

APRIL–SEPTEMBER

The distinguishing part of the lamb's-quarters, or goosefoot, is the diamond-shaped leaf. It looks like the webbed foot of a goose, sort of. Others declare that the leaf resembles a quarter of lamb. It is green-blue on top, with a white floury coating on top and bottom. Water runs off the plant or stands in droplets on the leaves.

The plant grows as tall as six or eight feet in some areas, and the whole plant is often tinted with red in the late summer.

Lamb's-quarters grows along roadsides and rail-roads, in cultivated fields and waste places all over the United States, but is most common in the Rockies and New England.

The leaves can be picked all season because they remain tender until the seeds set. Since the leaves boil down, gather about three times the amount you need.

The seeds are eaten by many game and songbirds and should be collected for your feeder. Nearly 75,000 seeds have been counted on a single plant, and the plants persist into the winter, which makes them a very valuable wildlife food.

The Navajos use the seeds for bread and pancakes. They dry them in the oven at a low heat, 200° F, until crisp, then pound them into a flour. Delicious added to oatmeal as a breakfast cereal.

LAMB'S-QUARTERS QUICHE

(Also good with chicory, plantain, dandelion flowers and/or greens.) Three cups of fresh lamb's-quarters leaves cook down to one cup. Boil fresh leaves in ¼ cup water for 10 minutes. Salt and drain. Chop into chunks. This will keep in refrigerator, covered, for several days.

Oven: 450°F, then 350°F

June–September

Time: 25 minutes

Ingredients
- 1 9″ pie crust
- 4 strips bacon
- 1 onion, thinly sliced
- 1 cup cubed Swiss cheese
- ¼ cup Parmesan cheese, grated
- 1 cup cooked, chopped lamb's-quarters
- 4 eggs, lightly beaten
- 2 cups cream, or 1 cup milk and 1 cup cream
- ¼ teaspoon nutmeg
- ½ teaspoon salt
- ¼ teaspoon white pepper

Utensils
- 9″ pie plate
- Cookie sheet
- Skillet
- Measuring cup
- Measuring spoons
- Mixing bowl
- Eggbeater

Directions

1. Bake pie crust 5 minutes. Place on cookie sheet.
2. Cook the bacon until crisp, remove from skillet, and drain.
3. Pour off all but 1 tablespoon of remaining fat from skillet.
4. Cook the onion in the tablespoon of fat until transparent.
5. Crumble the bacon.
6. Place onion, cheeses, lamb's-quarters, and bacon into pie crust.
7. Combine eggs, cream, nutmeg, salt, and pepper. Beat with eggbeater to mix.
8. Pour into pie crust.
9. Bake the pie 15 minutes. Reduce oven to 350°F. Bake about 10 minutes more, until a knife inserted 1 inch from the pastry edge comes out clean.
10. Serve hot.

SWEET AND SOUR
LAMB'S-QUARTERS

Ingredients
  2 strips bacon
  1 cup minced chives or
     onions
  1 tablespoon flour
  6 cups lamb's-quarters
     Water
  ¾ cup lamb's-quarters
     cooking liquid
  ¼ cup cider vinegar
  2 teaspoons sugar
  1 teaspoon salt
     Freshly ground pepper

Utensils
Skillet
Paper toweling
Measuring cup
Measuring
  spoons
2 bowls
Colander
2 3-quart
  saucepans

Directions
  1. Fry bacon in skillet until crisp. Drain bacon
     on paper toweling. Leave bacon fat in pan.
  2. Cook minced chives or onions in bacon
     fat about 5 minutes.
  3. Stir in flour, to make a paste.
  4. Cook lamb's-quarters 10 minutes in sauce-
     pan with ½ cup water and drain water into
     bowl through colander. Save the liquid and
     set lamb's-quarters aside.

5. In the same saucepan combine ¾ cup liquid from greens with vinegar, salt, sugar, and pepper. Heat on medium burner.
6. Add the onion-and-flour mix, and stir.
7. Add lamb's-quarters, and stir until mixture thickens.
8. Cook 2 more minutes.
9. Place in serving dish.
10. Crumble bacon on top.

OXALIS

SCIENTIFIC NAME: *Oxalis* (VARIOUS SPECIES)

APRIL–SEPTEMBER

*The cloverlike leaves of the lemon-flavored oxalis—
sorrel, sour grass, or Irish shamrock—make them easy
to recognize. The single flowers grow on stalks and
are a clear yellow.*

*The most common oxalis, yellow sorrel, grows from
Florida to New Mexico and all the way to Vermont.
I have found the common oxalis growing in the cracks
of city streets from New York to Denver, and the edge
of my garden is a veritable sour grass field in late
May.*

*The large yellow wood sorrel is coarser, with larger
blossoms, and thrives in the woods, especially on moist
mountaintops from Illinois and Pennsylvania south.*

OXALIS BROTH

Ingredients

1 teaspoon butter

4 cups sorrel (leaves, stems, and flowers)

5 cups of water and 5 chicken bouillon cubes, or 5 cups chicken broth

4 egg yolks

2 cups light cream

Utensils

Skillet

Measuring cup

Measuring spoons

3-quart saucepan

Small bowl

Whisk

Directions

1. Sauté sorrel in the butter until wilted. Set aside.
2. Pour 5 cups water in saucepan and bring to a boil.
3. Add bouillon cubes and stir until dissolved.
4. In small bowl, lightly beat together egg yolks and cream.
5. Remove broth from heat. Add the egg mixture, stirring with a whisk.
6. Return to heat and cook over low heat until slightly thickened, stirring constantly. Do not allow to boil.
7. Remove from heat.
8. Add sorrel and serve hot. Decorate with fresh sorrel leaves and flowers.
9. Marvelous broth. Also excellent icy cold.

BUILD AN OXALIS SANDWICH

Ingredients
½ cup oxalis
 2 slices bread of your
   choice
   Sliced cucumbers
   Sardines
   Crushed Fritos
   Mayonnaise
   Butter

Utensils
Top of kitchen
   table
Knife

Directions
1. Butter bread.
2. Cover one slice with mayonnaise.
3. Sprinkle with oxalis.
4. Pile on crushed Fritos, sardines, cucumbers, and anything else you like such as peanuts, green olives, and/or cheese.

PLANTAIN

SCIENTIFIC NAME: *Plantago major*
AND *P. lanceolata*
APRIL–NOVEMBER

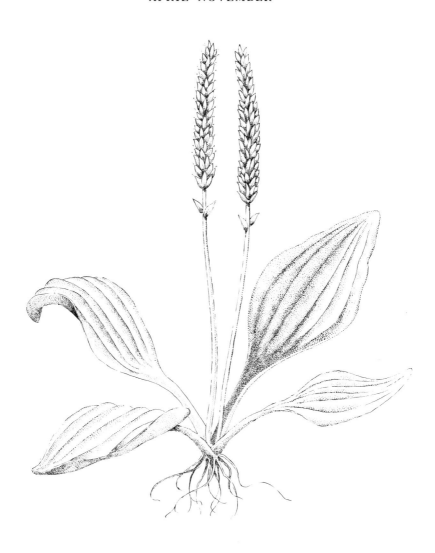

Plantain is a tough plant that prefers lawns and fields but can survive in sidewalk cracks, railroad beds, and other places where little else will grow. Broad leaves close to the ground spread out in a rosette and have strong stringlike fibers running from the foot-stalk to the tip of the leaf. The ribs are vertical, the flowers greenish or drab bronze, growing on a spike.

The seaside plantain, which has longer leaves, is coveted by the fishermen of the New England coast. The green can be cooked as potage (see "Dandelion Crowns") or served raw in a salad (see "Weedy Lawn Salad").

PURSLANE

SCIENTIFIC NAME: *Portulaca oleracea*

MAY–SEPTEMBER

The fat, fleshy leaves of the low-growing purslane are opposite each other. This and their tart taste are the best clues for identifying the delicious plant. The flowers, usually yellow, bloom at the forking of the stems and open only in bright sunshine. The podlike seed capsules have lids that open like gates, giving the plant its genus name, Portulaca, meaning gate or door. All parts of the plant can be eaten, but the flower buds and leaves are best.

This species of purslane grows all over the United States as well as in the warmer parts of Canada. Rich in vitamins and minerals, it is often grown in window boxes; the seeds can be ordered from catalogues. Fresh snippings add a taste sparkle to salads.

BAKED PURSLANE

Oven: 350° F   *Time: 30–35 minutes*

Ingredients

2 cups purslane leaves, freshly snipped from plant
1 cup dry bread crumbs
¼ teaspoon salt
¼ teaspoon pepper
1 egg, well beaten

Utensils

Mixing bowl
Measuring cup
Measuring spoon
Eggbeater
4-cup greased casserole

Directions

1. Toss together purslane, bread crumbs, salt, and pepper.
2. Stir in the well-beaten egg.
3. Pour into greased casserole.
4. Bake 35 minutes in 350°F oven.

Purslane is also an excellent rock-oven or campfire dish. Put the purslane in aluminum foil, sprinkle with salt, pepper, and butter, wrap well, and cook for 20 minutes.

SPICE BUSH

SCIENTIFIC NAME: *Lindera benzoin*

MARCH–MAY FOR FLOWERS

JULY–SEPTEMBER FOR FRUITS

A spicy-scented shrub with elliptic leaves. The stalked flowers are small, yellow-green, and appear in woodlands before the leaves of other trees come out, about the same time as the forsythia. They are easiest to recognize when flowering, and this is a good time to gather twigs and mark the tree with a ribbon for the autumn. The red berries make an excellent spice.

The bush grows in forests in rich fertile land. If you are in doubt as to the identification of spice bush, break off a twig and taste it. The flavor is a cross between spearmint and clove.

SPICE BUSH TEA

Ingredients

12 4-inch twigs of spice
    bush with flowers and
    leaves, or 1 cup berries
 2 quarts water
¼ cup sugar or honey
    (optional)

Utensils

3-quart saucepan
Colander
Measuring cup

Directions

1. Boil twigs in water with sugar or honey for 10 or 15 minutes.
2. Cool, strain, and place liquid in refrigerator.
3. Drink with ice or hot with sugar and milk.

SPICE BUSH SPICE

1. Gather the flowers in spring and the red fruits in autumn.
2. Place flowers or fruits on cookie sheet.
3. Bake in 275°F oven until dry.
4. Break into pieces and store.

Excellent on fish or added to vegetables and salads.

SPRING BEAUTY

SCIENTIFIC NAME: *Claytonia virginica* (EAST)
C. lanceolata (WEST)
APRIL–JUNE

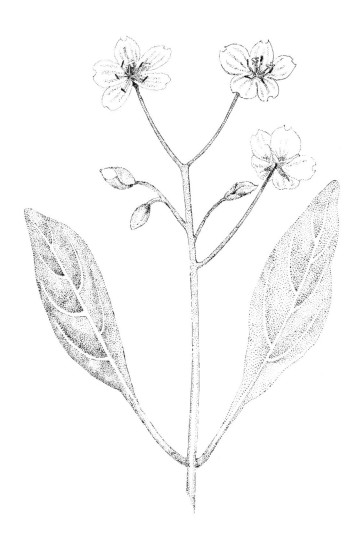

The spring beauty is among the first whitish or pinkish flowers to bloom in the spring. A pair of long opposite leaves folds back from the stem; each flower has five petals. The spring beauty grows from a round tuberlike core or nut, which is the edible portion of the plant. It grows on the floor of moist forests and shaded lawns in the East and up to 10,000 feet in the Rockies.

The nuts taste like radishes when eaten raw and like chestnuts when cooked. They lie deep in the ground, so take a shovel or trowel when you go foraging for them. The leaves, which are good as a potherb, can also be added raw to Weedy Lawn Salad.

MASHED SPRING BEAUTY
POTATOES

These tasty ground nuts should be used sparingly as they are a beautiful native plant. I serve them on special occasions, less than once every four or five years.

Ingredients
  2 cups spring beauty
    nuts
    Water
  2 tablespoons butter
  ½ cup milk
    Salt
    Pepper

Utensils
3-cup saucepan
Colander
Measuring cup
Measuring spoon
Potato masher

Directions
1. Boil spring beauty nuts in water until tender, about 25 minutes.
2. Drain.
3. Add butter, milk, and salt.
4. Mash until well mixed.
5. Sprinkle with pepper. Serve hot.

SUGAR MAPLE

SCIENTIFIC NAME: *Acer saccharum*

FEBRUARY–MARCH

It is best to locate your sugar maple tree in spring, summer, or autumn and tie a string around it until the end of March or early February, when the trees are tapped. Sugar maples are not as easy to identify when leafless.

To begin with, note whether or not the tree has opposite twigs on the branches. If so, you have one of the many maples. To identify the sugar-giving tree, note the leaves. The leaves of the sugar maple are large, with five deep, long-pointed lobes—the leaf on the Canadian flag. The leaves turn deep red, orange, and yellow in autumn and set the hills aflame. The bark is dark brown, marked with rough vertical grooves and ridges. Another identifying feature is that the flowers appear in spring just as the leaves come out. They are bell-shaped, yellow-green, and hang on slender strings. The maple keys or fruits of this tree ripen in the autumn and spin to the ground like whizzing propellers. They are sticky, and when the seed coat is split open they will stick to the nose like a rhinoceros horn.

Sugar maples seek the moist uplands and fertile valleys. Those growing in the north make the best syrup because the cold freezing nights send the sap back down the tree. This raises the sugar content.

BACKYARD MAPLE SYRUP

Utensils

Hand-bit brace for drilling into maple tree

$\frac{7}{16}''$ bit drill to fit hand-bit brace (An electric drill, if outlet is available)

12 cement blocks to make fire box

Scraps and split wood (½ cord of wood is good for 5 gallons of syrup.)

Large baking pan or lasagne pan

10 to 20 1-gallon plastic milk bottles with lids and handles

10 to 20 spyles (metal or wooden troughs down which sap runs into bucket. Steel spyles can be purchased in hardware store, wooden ones can be made. See directions below.)

Pitcher for pouring into bottles.

Funnel

Cup

Directions

1. Arrange the cement blocks with 2 open ends and just far enough apart to support the large baking pan. The pan can sit on the top of the blocks but preferably should be nestled down into them to keep the wind from cooling the sap. Stack cord wood near

fire box and cover with plastic to keep dry. Wash gallon plastic bottles.

2. When the February days are above freezing and the nights are below, it is time to tap your maple trees.

3. Drill holes, 2½″ deep, preferably over large roots or below a healthy limb that is pulling sap. The best runs come from the south to southwest sides of a trunk. Drill hole slightly uphill so that sap flows outward. Remove shavings.

4. Insert spyle.

5. Hang milk bottles on spyle by handle. Mark where the spyle hits the bottle and cut a hole. Hang bottle over spyle. Tap other trees. A big tree can hold 4 or 5 buckets.

6. You can make spyles by drilling a hole in a ½″ dowel about 4″ long. These spyles will need a little whittling to fit.

7. When the milk bottles are full, start up the fire. Pour sap in evaporating or baking pan. Thirty-three gallons of sap will yield 1 gallon of syrup.

8. Keep fires going until sap has boiled down into syrup. About 6 hours will do it.

9. Cool and store in bottles, coffee cans, or jugs.

10. Maple syruping calls for lots of improvisation. Use all kinds of equipment, even the kitchen stove, although the long boiling process does steam up the kitchen.

MAPLE SYRUP
BLACK WALNUT CAKE

Oven: 325°F   *Time: 1½ hours*

Ingredients

2 sticks butter or margarine
¼ cup cooking oil
1 cup brown sugar
2 cups white sugar
5 eggs, beaten
½ cup self-rising flour
2½ cups plain flour
1 cup milk
1½ cups black walnuts
1 teaspoon vanilla
1 teaspoon maple syrup

Utensils

Large mixing bowl
Mixing spoon
Measuring cup
Measuring spoons
8" x 8" square cake pan, greased
Cake rack

Directions

1. Cream butter, cooking oil, and sugars.
2. Add beaten eggs.
3. Alternately add flours and milk.
4. Add black walnuts, vanilla, and maple syrup.
5. Bake in preheated oven at 325°F for 1½ hours.
6. Let the cake set for 15 minutes.
7. Turn out onto cake rack. Let cool.

VIOLET

SCIENTIFIC NAMES: *Violaceae* (VARIOUS KINDS)

APRIL–MAY FOR FLOWERS

ALL YEAR FOR LEAVES

The heart-shaped leaf of the common blue violet, Viola papilionacea, *is a real giveaway. The flowers of these low plants suggest tiny pansies with their five petals. They vary in color from white through yellows to blues and purples. All are delicious, both leaves and flowers, but the purple ones have the sweetest taste. The roots are not so good. Some violet leaves are deeply segmented, like fingers on hands; these are less tasty. Those with heart-shaped leaves are best. The flowers are a rich source of Vitamin C.*

VIOLET LEAVES AND BUTTER

Ingredients
  3 cups young violet
    leaves
  ¼ cup water
  ¼ teaspoon salt
  1 tablespoon butter

Utensils
Colander
3-quart saucepan
Measuring cup
Measuring
  spoons
Mixing spoon

Directions
1. Wash and drain violet leaves.
2. Bring water to a boil.
3. Add violet leaves and salt.
4. Turn heat down to medium, cover, and simmer for 5 minutes.
5. Drain and serve with butter.

SUGARED VIOLETS

Oven: 200°F   *Time: 40 minutes*

Ingredients   *Utensils*
1 or 2 egg whites   2 bowls
1 box superfine   Cookie sheet
   granulated sugar   Waxed paper
Several dozen violets with   Toothpicks
   long stems   Spatula or
            tweezers
            Cloth to wipe
              fingers

Directions
1. Beat the egg white until frothy.
2. Pour superfine sugar in the other bowl.
3. Cover cookie sheet with waxed paper.
4. Pick up a violet by the stem and dip in egg white.
5. Dip into granulated sugar until flower is sugared top and bottom.
6. Place on cookie sheet. Using a toothpick, straighten the petals.
7. Repeat until all the violets are dipped. Leave stems as handles to help you remove them from paper.
8. Place in oven for about 40 minutes or until the sugar crystalizes. It turns frosty white.

9. While they're cooking, unroll another piece of waxed paper.
10. When sugar is crystallized, lift violets off cookie sheet with spatula, tweezers, or fingers and place on second piece of waxed paper.
11. If the flowers look wet and glisteny, sprinkle with more sugar.
12. Cool for about an hour.
13. Cut off stems.
14. Store in airtight cookie or candy box. Place waxed paper between layers. Sugared violets will keep in this manner for a year or more.
15. Serve as candy or as a top for desserts, fruit salads, and ice cream.

Forsythia, pear, and apple blossoms can also be sugared and preserved, but violets are best. They are sturdier and more perfumy.

VIOLET LEAF SOUP

Ingredients

 4 cups violet leaves
 1 small onion, chopped
 1 small wild garlic and
   bits of chopped wild
   garlic greens
   (optional)
 2 tablespoons butter
1½ cups water
 2 bouillon cubes
   Salt
   Pepper

Utensils

Measuring cup
Measuring
  spoons
Colander
Chopping board
Chopping knife
9″ frying pan
3-quart saucepan
Mixing spoon

Directions

1. Rinse and drain violet leaves.
2. Chop onion, wild garlic bud, and garlic tops.
3. Place butter in frying pan.
4. Melt the butter.
5. Place violet leaves, onions, and garlic bud in pan.
6. Cover and simmer for 10 minutes.
7. Pour water over mixture. Heat slowly.
8. Add bouillon cubes, and heat until they dissolve.
9. Salt and pepper to taste.

10. Garnish with the chopped green garlic tops.
11. Serve in soup bowls adorned with violet flowers.

WILD GINGER

SCIENTIFIC NAME: *Asarum canadense*

MAY–JUNE

The leaves of the wild ginger plant are heart-shaped, large—about three to four inches—with hairy stems. The flower is tucked shyly between two leaves that grow out from a single stem. In the crotch between the leaf stalks is a single odd and mysterious purple-brown flower. It is cup-shaped, with three pointed red-brown calyx leaves. Since the leaf stems fork close to the ground, the flower is often hiding under the leaves.

The wild ginger is found in rich woods at the base of bluffs and in ravines from Minnesota to the Gaspé and south to Arkansas and North Carolina.

You are after the long rootstocks. They should be dug with a shovel—they are deep. They can be used as a spice—dry, raw, or cooked. Use twice as much as the standard tropical ginger, which is stronger. Hang roots to dry, or spread on cookie sheets and roast two or three hours in a 300° F oven.

71

CANDIED WILD GINGER

Ingredients
 8 to 10 roots of ginger
  plant, cut into short
  pieces
 1 cup maple syrup
 1 cup sugar
½ cup water
 Granulated sugar

Utensils
Vegetable brush
Measuring cup
3-quart saucepan
Waxed paper

Directions
1. Wash ginger root pieces thoroughly.
2. Drop ginger into mix of syrup, sugar, and water, and bring to a slow boil.
3. Boil about 1 hour or until soft and well done.
4. Place on waxed paper and cool.
5. Sprinkle with granulated sugar.
6. Store in candy jar for nibbles.

GINGER SPICE

1. Chop the root and use fresh as a spice with fish and meats.

   or

1. Wash roots thoroughly and lay on cookie sheet.
2. Bake until dry at 275°F.
3. Crush with hammer or in a coffee-bean grinder until a powder.
4. Use in sauces and curries.

SUMMER

CHICORY

SCIENTIFIC NAME: *Cichorium intybus*

MAY–JULY FOR PLANTS

ALL YEAR FOR ROOTS

Chicory's blue flowers are unmistakable, gleaming along roadsides, railroad beds and in abandoned fields. They have no stalks and just erupt from the stem. The flowers, which are square-tipped and fringed, open at sun-up and are closed by noon. The bottom leaves lie against the ground and look like dandelion leaves. These are edible, especially when they are young and tender, and can be mixed with dandelion greens and plantain for salad. (See Weedy Lawn Salad.)

Roots, washed, baked in a 200°F oven, and ground, make delicious coffee.

CHICORY SANDWICH

Ingredients

1½ cups washed chicory
  leaves
 4 cups water
 4 strips bacon, diced
 3 tablespoons lemon
  juice or vinegar
 2 teaspoons sugar
 6 slices bread
 ¼ cup grated cheese of
  your choice

Utensils

Measuring cup
Measuring
  spoons
3-quart saucepan
Colander
Large skillet
Griddle or
  broiler

Directions

1. In saucepan, place chicory in water and boil 5 minutes.
2. Drain off water.
3. Fry bacon in skillet until crisp. Remove and drain on toweling. Save bacon fat.
4. Add cooked chicory to bacon fat and fry for 10 minutes.
5. Add lemon juice or vinegar. Stir.
6. Add sugar. Stir.
7. Over low heat, cook and stir for 3 minutes.
8. Turn out on 3 pieces of toast
9. Sprinkle with cheese.

10. Set under broiler and brown.
    or
11. Press on other slices of bread as sandwich tops and fry until brown on griddle or skillet. Turn once.

MEXICAN GREEN SPOON BREAD

Oven: 400° F   *Time: 45 minutes*

Ingredients

1-pound can creamy-style corn

¾ cup melted butter, bacon fat, or chicken fat

3 large eggs

¾ cup milk

1 cup coarsely ground cornmeal

½ teaspoon baking soda

1 teaspoon salt

1 cup grated cheddar cheese

1 medium onion, chopped

½ cup cooked chopped chicory, dandelion greens, or oxalis

Utensils

2 bowls

Measuring cup

Measuring spoon

Mixing spoon

Grater

Greased 9" square baking pan or bread pan

Directions

1. In a large bowl, combine the corn, milk, butter, and eggs.
2. In other bowl, blend together the cornmeal, soda, and salt.
3. Stir dry ingredients into liquid mixture a bit at a time, and blend well.
4. Put half the batter into greased 9″ square pan.
5. Spread with one half of the grated cheese, onions, and cooked chopped chicory.
6. Add rest of batter.
7. Top with remainder of the cheese, onion, and chicory.
8. Bake in a 400°F oven 45 minutes or until brown.
9. Cool slightly before spooning.

DAY LILY

SCIENTIFIC NAME: *Hemerocallis*
(VARIOUS SPECIES)
JULY–AUGUST FOR BUDS AND FLOWERS
SEPTEMBER–NOVEMBER FOR ROOTS

Perky orange and yellow flowers with six petals. They bloom in high summer face up to the sun. The flowers are clustered on the top of a naked stalk. They last but one day, opening at dawn and closing in the evening. The leaves are long and lancelike. This is not a lily with a bulb, as are the trillium, onion, tulip and hyacinth, etc., but a member of the Lily Family with a root, an alien of Asiatic origin. The plant came to America via Europe, and escaped from gardens to the roadsides and woodland meadows across the eastern United States. It has migrated now to moist western wastelands.

The buds, the open flowers, the wilted flowers, and the roots are good to eat, and are considered delicacies in Japan and China. Boil roots in salt water and serve with butter, or use in Fiddlehead Pie.

LEMON DAY LILIES

Ingredients
- 2 dozen day lily buds or wilted flowers
- 4 cups water
- ¾ cup sugar
- ½ cup white vinegar
- 1 cup canned chicken broth
- 1 lemon, juice and grated rind
- 1 tablespoon cornstarch
- 2 tablespoons water
- Cooked rice
- Candied wild ginger (see page 72.)

Utensils
- Measuring cup
- Measuring spoon
- 3-quart saucepan
- Colander
- Grater
- Lemon squeezer
- Bowl

Directions
1. Boil day lilies in water for 15 minutes.
2. Drain.
3. Pour sugar and vinegar in saucepan. Heat until dissolved.
4. Add chicken broth. Stir.
5. Add lemon juice and grated rind. Stir.
6. Simmer for 5 minutes.
7. Dissolve cornstarch in 2 tablespoons water. Add to sauce.

8. Over low heat, stir constantly until thickened and clear.
9. Add day lilies. Heat briefly.
10. Serve over rice with sliced candied wild ginger.

DAY LILY FRITTERS

Ingredients

12 buds or wilted flowers of day lilies
4 cups water
1 cup biscuit mix
¾ cup water or milk (enough to make pasty mixture)

or in lieu of biscuit mix

1 cup flour
2 eggs, well beaten
⅔ cup milk
1 teaspoon baking powder
¼ teaspoon salt
Pepper
½ inch cooking oil in skillet

Utensils

Measuring cup
Measuring spoons
3-quart saucepan
Bowl
Mixing spoon
Skillet
Paper toweling or brown paper bag

Directions

1. Place day lilies and water in saucepan and bring to boil.
2. Simmer for 15 minutes.
3. Drain cooked lilies and pat dry. Dip into batter.
4. Drop into hot fat and cook until golden brown.
5. Turn and cook other side.
6. Drain on paper toweling or brown paper bag.
7. Serve as vegetable or snack.

WILD BLACK CHERRY

SCIENTIFIC NAME: *Prunus serotina*

JUNE–OCTOBER

The flowers of the wild black cherry open from the end of March in Texas to June in the North, are about one half inch in diameter, and hang in clusters. They appear when the leaves are half grown. The fruits ripen from June to October in drooping clusters and are round and bright red when fully grown, and almost black when ripe.

The bark is broken into scaly small irregular plates that are dark cherry red.

This tree grows from Nova Scotia westward to Lake Superior and southward to Florida, Nebraska, South Dakota, Kansas, Oklahoma, and the Rio River, Texas, usually in rich soil. They were once abundant in the Appalachian Mountains.

CHERRY CORN BREAD

Ingredients
1 cup cherries
2 cups water
2 tablespoons honey

Utensils
Measuring cup
Measuring
  spoons
3-quart saucepan
Colander

Directions
1. Place cherries and water in saucepan.
2. Bring to a boil and simmer for 20 minutes.
3. Drain juice through colander and reserve.
4. Pit the cherries—give a little squeeze and the seeds pop out.
5. Combine pitted cherries and honey.

THE BREAD:

Oven: 425°F

Time: 20–30 minutes

Ingredients
1 cup cornmeal
1 cup whole wheat flour
2 teaspoons baking
  powder
1 teaspoon salt
1 egg

Utensils
9" cake pan
2 mixing bowls
Measuring cup
Measuring
  spoons

Ingredients (cont.)

1 tablespoon honey
2 tablespoons melted
   margarine, butter, or
   cooking oil
1 tablespoon sugar
   Juice from 1 cup of
   cooked cherries
   Water
1 cup cherries, prepared
   as above

Directions

1. Grease a 9″ cake pan and put in oven to heat.
2. Combine cornmeal, flour, baking powder, and salt.
3. In second bowl, stir together egg, honey, and melted margarine or cooking oil.
4. Pour cherry liquid into measuring cup and add water to make ¾ cup. Add to egg mixture.
5. Mix dry ingredients with egg mixture.
6. Stir in cherries.
7. Pour batter into hot pan and bake at 425°F for 20 to 30 minutes, or when browned and toothpick comes out clean after being inserted.

Also use raspberries, gooseberries, blueberries and relatives; rose hips, high bush cranberries, manzanitas.

Wild black cherries may be used as a substitute fruit in elderberry recipes.

WILD CHERRY BREAKFAST CAKE

Oven: 425°F,
or put in coals or rock oven

Time: 20–25 minutes

Ingredients
  2 cups biscuit mix
⅔ cup milk
  2 tablespoons sugar
  1 egg
  1 cup wild cherries,
     pitted and sweetened
     with honey
     Honey, butter or maple
     syrup.

Utensils
Bowl
Measuring cup
Measuring
   spoons
Mixing spoon
Cake pan

Directions
1. Pour biscuit mix into bowl.
2. Add milk. Stir.
3. Add sugar. Stir.
4. Stir in egg.
5. Fold in wild cherries
6. Bake 20 to 25 minutes.
7. Serve with honey, butter, or maple syrup.

BLUEBERRIES

AND VARIOUS RELATIVES

SCIENTIFIC NAME: *Vaccinium*
(VARIOUS SPECIES)
AUGUST

DESCRIPTION AND HABITAT

Blueberries, huckleberries, bilberries, deerberries, and cranberries are members of the Heath family. All belong to the genus **Vaccinium** *and resemble each other rather closely. Blueberries have small elliptical leaves with short stems, and their twigs are covered with numerous raised warts. The bell-like flowers are small and whitish and the fruits can be anywhere from blue to black. They contain many small seeds. Huckleberries, on the other hand, have exactly ten seeds per fruit. The other* **Vaccinium** *look much the same as these two famous members of the group. All are edible.*

Locate your blueberry and huckleberry patches in the spring and summer on mountainsides, in pine forests and abandoned fields, then gather them in midsummer before the bears and birds get them.

Each species seeks out a different habitat where it will not compete with others of its kind. The highbush blueberry has adapted to wet or barren sites, the low bush blueberry makes a home in dry woods and thickets. The bilberry grows in tundra bogs and stony ground, while the deerberry has adapted to open woods and forest openings. I find these bushes while walking on trails and mark them down on a geological survey map for harvesting in their seasons.

Use blueberries and various relatives in elderberry and wild cherry recipes.

HIGH BUSH CRANBERRY

SCIENTIFIC NAME: *Viburnum trilobum*

JULY–AUGUST

The three-lobed leaf, which tends to be long-pointed, is a distinguishing feature of this tall shrub. Its twigs are hairless, its flowers white clusters that bloom in May and June and the berries are ready to harvest in late July and through August. A delicious tart fruit, this species is used as a substitute for the true cranberry, the large American cranberry Vaccinium macrocarpon, *which is a slender-stemmed plant with leaves that are oblong, blunt at the tip, and slightly whitish underneath.*

Use High Bush Cranberry as a substitute fruit in Wild Cherry and Elderberry recipes.

ELDERBERRY

SCIENTIFIC NAMES: *Sambucus callicarpa,*
Sambucus canadensis, ALSO *S. melanacarpa* AND
S. mexicana IN THE SOUTHWEST

JULY–OCTOBER

This shrub, three to thirteen feet tall, looks much the same whether it grows in the East or the West. The large leaves are composed of five to eleven coarse-toothed leaflets that make up one big leaf. The twigs are stout with large white pithy centers, the best identifying characteristic.

The white flowers grow in dense, flat-topped clusters. Fruits are also flat-topped, each berry being less than $\frac{3}{16}$ th of an inch. They are juicy and are usually purple-black when ripe, although some western species are dark red. Foxes, squirrels, and moose enjoy elderberries, so watch for them.

Elderberry bushes are found along washes and streams across the country and in the West on slopes where there is adequate moisture. Look along roadsides, near culverts, and along streams.

ELDERBERRY TART

(also blueberry, huckleberry, raspberry, manzanita, wild cherry)

Oven: 350°F   *Time: 30–40 minutes*

FABULOUS CRUST

Ingredients

1 cup flour
½ cup butter
  Rind grated from one
  lemon
  Egg yolk

Utensils

Mixing bowl
Measuring cup
Measuring
  spoons
Grater
Floured cutting
  board
Rolling pin
9″ pie plate
Lemon squeezer

Directions

1. Mix flour, butter, rind, and egg yolk with hands until creamy.
2. Roll into a ball.
3. Refrigerate until chilled (about 1 hour).
4. Put dough on floured board and roll flat.
5. Place crust in pie plate.

¾ cup sugar

½ teaspoon cinnamon

Juice from ½ lemon

3 cups elderberry or other fruit

2 tablespoons butter

Directions

1. In bowl, mix sugar, cinnamon, and lemon juice.
2. Place three cups of elderberry or other fruit in pie crust.
3. Pour sugar mix over fruit.
4. Dot with butter.
5. Bake in 350°F oven 30 to 40 minutes or until crust is brown.
6. Serve hot with ice cream or whipped cream.

This filling can also be used in store-made pie crusts or biscuit-mix pie crusts, but the pie crust should be browned slightly before adding fruits.

MILK PUNCH WITH ELDERBERRY FLOWERS

June

Ingredients

1 quart milk
8 clusters elderberry flowers snipped from stems, washed, patted dry on toweling
½ lemon, squeezed for juice, the rind cut up very fine or pulverized in blender
3 tablespoons honey
Grated nutmeg

Utensils

Cutting board
Sharp knife
Blender (optional)
Measuring spoons
3-quart saucepan
1½-quart pitcher
Tea strainer
Lemon squeezer

Directions

1. In saucepan heat milk to boiling point, but do not boil.
2. Put elderberry flowers, lemon juice, and rind in pitcher.
3. Pour hot milk over flowers.
4. Add honey.
5. Stir. Cool in refrigerator.
6. Strain and serve in glasses or cups.
7. Sprinkle with nutmeg.

MANZANITAS

SCIENTIFIC NAME: *Arctostaphylos*
(VARIOUS SPECIES).
Arctostaphylos glaucae
HAS THE LARGEST BERRIES.
JULY–NOVEMBER

Manzanitas are evergreen shrubs of the Pacific coast states. They are very dense and spread out in tight tangles that shelter gamebirds, song birds, and small mammals. The red bark, pointed oval leaves, and crooked branches make these trees easy to recognize.

Manzanita is the Spanish name for "little apple," a perfect name, for the fruit does look just like a little apple.

Along the Pacific coast the manzanitas grow profusely on dry ridges from the lowlands to the mountain tops. Two or three species grow in southern Utah, Colorado, Arizona, New Mexico, and Mexico. Raccoons and skunks feast on them, and the black-tailed and mule deer browse on these plants extensively.

The West Coast Indians eat the fruits raw, cooked, as jelly, or as a beverage. The seeds are ground into a mush.

MANZANITA PUNCH

Ingredients
4 cups washed manzanita
  berries
4 cups water

Utensils
6-quart saucepan
Strainer
Potato masher
Bowl
Pitcher

Directions

1. Place manzanita berries in saucepan and add water.
2. Simmer gently for 15 minutes. Do not boil.
3. Drain the berries; reserve the liquid.
4. Mash the berries with a potato masher.
5. Measure fruit.
6. Put fruit in bowl, and add as much fruit liquid as you have fruit.
7. Let mixture settle for a day.
8. Strain off liquid, discard the berries, and refrigerate the juice.
9. Let settle again.
10. Serve in glasses with ice. Sweeten if desired.

Mix with other wild teas and juices for fascinating tastes. Use with seeded berries in Elderberry Tart recipe. Reserve juice for jelly.

MANZANITA JELLY

Ingredients

4 cups manzanita punch
7 cups sugar
1 pouch fruit pectin

Utensils

4 or 5 jelly jars
12-quart pot for
    boiling jars
Measuring cup
Bowl
Mixing spoon
4-quart saucepan
Paraffin
Small pan to melt
    paraffin

Directions

1. Sterilize jars in pot of boiling water 5 minutes.
2. Combine fruit juice and sugar.
3. Stir in pectin.
4. In saucepan, bring to a boil and simmer 5 minutes—no more.
5. Pour into sterilized jars.
6. Cover with melted paraffin.

MILKWEED

SCIENTIFIC NAME: *Asclepias syriaca*

JUNE–AUGUST

This plant, with its stout stem and bold oval leaves, has domed pink flower clusters. The plants grow two to five feet high. A milky substance flows from all parts of the plant when they are broken—leaves, stems, and flowers.

Collect buds from the milkweed in June before the flowers open. Return in five to ten days to pick the tiny pods. They should be from one-half inch to less than one inch. Any bigger and they are filled with fuzz.

A bonus in foraging for this plant is that the monarch butterfly lays its tiny (pin-head sized) white, barrel-shaped eggs on the underside of the leaves. The monarchs lay and feed only on milkweeds. Look for the eggs and/or the black, orange, and white caterpillar. Bring eggs, larva, and plant home. Place the plant in a jug of water to keep it fresh. As the caterpillars grow, gather fresh leaves. Monarch caterpillars turn to an exquisite green chrysalis in ten to fifteen days. Watch the caterpillars when they are restless, and confine them to a large lidded jar with sticks on which to pupate. About twelve days later, when the chrysalis is dark red-brown and you can see the butterfly inside, check every fifteen minutes to observe the metamorphosis, the emergence of a gorgeous butterfly, an inspiring sight.

MILKWEED BUDS

Ingredients
Water
4 or 5 cups milkweed buds
3 tablespoons olive oil
1 tablespoon vinegar
Salt

Utensils
12-quart pot
Measuring cup
Measuring
spoons
Small pot

Directions
1. Boil large pot of water and keep it boiling.
2. Place milkweed in a small pot.
3. Cover with boiling water.
4. Boil 1 or 2 minutes and pour off water.
5. Repeat 2 or 3 times or until the bitterness is gone.
6. Pour into serving dish.
7. Serve with olive oil and vinegar. Salt to taste.
8. Eat hot or cold in salad.

MILKWEED PODS

Ingredients

1 cup small milkweed
  pods, ¼ " to ¾ " long,
  no more
Water
Butter
Salt
Pepper

Utensils

1-quart saucepan
Measuring cup

Directions

1. Place pods in saucepan. Cover with water and bring to a boil.
2. Simmer for 5 minutes.
3. Pour off water.
4. Add ½ cup water, and simmer 10 minutes.
5. Serve with butter, salt, and pepper.

MILKWEED POD PIE

Oven: 375° F   *Time: 20 minutes*

Ingredients

3 cups milkweed pods
  Water
2 tablespoons butter
2 tablespoons flour

Utensils

Colander
3-quart saucepan
Measuring cup
Mixing spoon

Ingredients (cont.)
1 cup milk
¼ teaspoon salt
1 baked pie shell
Grated Parmesan
cheese or grated
cheese of your choice.
(I like Vermont
cheddar.)

Utensils (cont.)
Measuring
spoons

Directions

1. Cover and boil milkweed pods in water 5 minutes, change water, boil 10 more minutes. Drain.
2. Stir in and melt butter.
3. Add flour and stir until all pods are covered.
4. Add milk slowly, stirring all the time until mixture thickens.
5. Add salt.
6. Pour into baked pie shell.
7. Sprinkle with grated cheese.
8. Place in 375°F oven until mixture bubbles and cheese melts.
9. Devour.

PRICKLY PEAR

SCIENTIFIC NAME: *Opuntia phaecacantha*
AND *O. humifus*, PLUS ABOUT 100 OTHER
VARIETIES
JULY–AUGUST FOR FRUIT; ALL YEAR FOR PADS

Sometimes called "beaver tail" because of its flat round pads, the prickly pear is found in the desert areas throughout the West, and in wastelands in the East and Northeast. The prickly pear is easy to recognize for it is the symbol of the Southwest with its beaver tail upon beaver tail. Large, waxy flowers appear in the spring, followed by juicy red fruits.

Approximately forty-four gamebirds, songbirds, and mammals, including ring-tailed cat and coyote, eat these nourishing and delicious seeds and fruits. Bite into a sun-warmed fruit for a treat.

PRICKLY PEAR FRUIT JUICE

Gather the red fruits with tongs or gloves to avoid spines. The darker the fruit, the riper and juicier.

Utensils
  2 bowls
  3-quart saucepan
    Potato masher
    Colander and/or
    cheesecloth

Directions
1. To clean spines from pears (the Indians call them tunas), I use a tough pair of work gloves and rub them off under running water. Fill a medium-sized saucepan with water and bring to a boil.
2. Put pears in boiling water and cook for about 15 minutes.
3. Cool.
4. Slice pears in half and take out the seeds with thumb. Put pears in one bowl and seeds in another.
5. Mash the fruit pulp with a potato masher and strain through a colander or cheese cloth.

6. Pour juice into clean glasses and refrigerate.
7. Two dozen tunas yield about one quart of juice. The juice can be used to make jelly and punch. Use fruit as a substitute in Elderberry Tart.
8. Fry the seeds in butter for snacks.

PRICKLY PEAR JELLY

Ingredients

2½ cups prickly pear fruit
     juice
3½ cups sugar
  3 tablespoons lemon
     juice
  1 pouch fruit pectin

Utensils

4 or 5 jelly jars
12-quart pot for
     boiling jelly
     jars
Measuring cup
Measuring
     spoons
Lemon squeezer
Mixing spoon
4-quart saucepan
Paraffin
Small pan placed
     in larger pan of
     water to melt
     paraffin

Directions

1. Boil jelly jars 5 minutes.
2. Pour prickly pear fruit juice in pan.
3. Add sugar and lemon juice.
4. Heat and dissolve sugar.
5. Add pectin and place over heat, stirring constantly.
6. Bring to a hard boil for 3 minutes. Be sure to watch the time, because the pectin jells quickly.

7. Remove from heat.
8. Skim off foam.
9. Fill sterilized jars with jelly.
10. Melt paraffin.
11. Cover jelly with thin layer of melted paraffin, cool, and store jelly.

PRICKLY PEAR JELLY ROLL

Oven: 400°F   *Time: 10–15 minutes*

Ingredients   *Utensils*
  2 cups biscuit mix   Measuring cup
  ⅔ cup water   Mixing bowl
  1 cup prickly pear jelly   Mixing spoon
                                 Floured table or
                                     board
                                 Rolling pin
                                 Greased cookie
                                     sheet
                                 For camping,
                                     greased camp
                                     bucket and lid

Directions
1. Pour biscuit mix into bowl and add water.
2. Stir until well mixed and easy to handle. If sticky, add more mix.
3. Turn onto floured table or board.
4. Roll to about ½ inch thickness.
5. Spread prickly pear jelly on biscuit mix.
6. Roll lightly into loose roll.
7. Bake in preheated oven for 10 to 15 minutes or until brown.
8. Slice and serve with herbal tea from your region.

1. Place jelly roll in greased pot with lid.
2. Rake coals over and around pot.
3. Bake 15 minutes.

BAKED PRICKLY PEAR PADS

Oven: 375° F   *Time: 1 hour*

Using gloves carefully, cut about 8 or 10 prickly pear pads. The small new green pads are the tenderest. This plant is mucilagenous and although rich in vitamins needs to be doctored a bit.

Directions

1. Wrap the pads in aluminum foil. Sprinkle with a little water and bake for 1 hour.
2. Set aside until cool.
3. Remove skins and thorns. If cooked long enough both peel right off.
4. Remove any remaining spines with knife. Those around the edges can be cut with scissors.
5. Cut into long, thin strips. Store half the slices for other recipes.
6. Reheat and serve with butter and salt if you like texture that is gluey. Otherwise try the next recipe.

FRIED PRICKLY PEAR PADS

Ingredients
1 egg
½ teaspoon salt
Pepper
½ cup cornmeal
1 cup baked prickly pear
½ cup cooking oil
Small piece of bread

Utensils
Small bowl
Measuring cup
Measuring
  spoons
Eggbeater
Large platter
9″ frying pan
Fork or tongs

Directions
1. Beat egg in small bowl.
2. Add salt and pepper.
3. Pour cornmeal on platter.
4. Dip prickly pear strips in egg.
5. Roll strips in cornmeal.
6. Heat oil until it browns a small piece of bread.
7. Place prickly pear strips in oil.
8. Cook until brown.
9. Remove with tongs and serve hot.

PRICKLY PEAR PAD OMELET

Ingredients

 2 tablespoons finely
   chopped onion
 1 tablespoon oil or
   butter
 2 tablespoons diced,
   baked prickly pear pads
 4 eggs, beaten
 1 tablespoon water
½ teaspoon salt
   Pepper

Utensils

Measuring
  spoons
Heavy frying pan
Mixing bowl
Eggbeater
Mixing spoon
Pancake turner

Directions

1. Fry onions in butter until transparent.
2. Add prickly pear pads and heat thoroughly.
3. Beat together eggs, water, salt, and pepper until light.
4. Pour into frying pan with mix and scramble quickly.
5. Let bottom fry until brown.
6. Fold over and serve. Don't overcook.

RASPBERRIES AND BLACKBERRIES

SCIENTIFIC NAME: *Rubus* (VARIOUS SPECIES)

JUNE–AUGUST

STRAWBERRIES

SCIENTIFIC NAME: *Rubus* (VARIOUS SPECIES)

JUNE–AUGUST

All these luscious fruits are cousins and members of the Rose family. Like the rose they all have prickers, although strawberry prickers are rather soft. All have five-petalled flowers. The fruits are made up of many juicy drupelets, each containing a hard seed.

Strawberries grow along the ground while the other two grow in high tangles that sometimes cover great areas. They like poor soil along roads, railroads, and in abandoned fields.

One other member of this group, the thimbleberry, grows in the upper Great Lakes region and is a shrub rather than a briar patch. Its large leaves and showy flowers resemble wild roses. The fruits are big and luscious.

Eat fresh or use in pies, tarts, jellies, and punch.

123

AUTUMN

ACORNS

SCIENTIFIC NAME: *Quercus* (VARIOUS SPECIES)

SEPTEMBER–OCTOBER

Oaks, the makers of acorns, vary from huge spreading trees in the East to shrubs in the high dry mountains of the West. The brown shiny nut with its cap is the oak's best identification. Since white oak acorns are sweeter and have less tannin than the red oak acorns, seek out one of the many white oaks. Oaks are divided into two groups, the whites and the reds. The whites are smooth-lobed; they do not have hairlike bristle tips on the ends of the leaf lobes—with one exception, the chestnut oak.

More wild things eat acorns than any other food, not only because they are abundant, but because they are nutritious. Mark your trees in spring and summer and collect your acorns in late summer and early fall before the squirrels, deer, peccaries, blue jays, etc., etc. collect them.

All acorns are somewhat bitter with tannin, which is most easily removed by boiling.

ACORN FLOUR

Eight quarts, or 1 peck, of shelled acorns yield about 6 cups of acorn flour.

1. Place acorns in a 12-quart pot of water. Skim off those that float; they are hosts to the worm of the acorn borer *Curculio nasicus* and are not any good. Keep a few of the floaters in a jar of earth, the worms will come out, go into the ground, and in June or July a handsome beetle will be your guest.

2. Put the acorns that sink in a big pot, cover with water, and bring to a boil. Turn the heat down and simmer for 20 minutes to soften shell. Pour off the water and let the acorns cool.

3. With a metal nutcracker, crack the acorns from side to side, not top to bottom. The hulls will break in half and fall off.

4. When the acorns are husked, return them to the pot and cover with water once more. Bring to a boil and simmer for 20 minutes. Pour off the tannin-darkened water. Cover with fresh water and boil again.

5. Repeat this 4 or 5 times or until no more tannin comes out of the acorns. They will be dark. When the water boils clearly, taste an acorn to make sure it is not bitter. If bitter, boil until it is not.

Directions for baking flour   *Oven: 200°–300°F*

1. Spread acorns on a cookie sheet and place in oven.
2. Bake for 2 or 3 hours. When the kernels are dry and brittle, remove from oven and blow off chaff.
3. Grind to flour in an electric coffee mill, or pound in a wooden bowl.
4. Store acorn flour in glass jars or flour container for later use.

ACORN PANCAKES

Ingredients

½ cup white flour
1 cup acorn flour
2½ teaspoons baking powder
¾ teaspoon salt
1 egg, well beaten
1¼ cups milk, approximately
3 tablespoons butter or margarine melted and slightly cooled, or cooking oil

Utensils

2 mixing bowls
Measuring spoons
Measuring cup
Eggbeater
Mixing spoon
Griddle or skillet
Pancake turner

Ingredients (cont.)

Optional: ½ cup blueberries, elderberries, wild cherries, prickly pear fruits, or other wild fruit.

Maple syrup, wild jams or jellies

Directions

1. In one bowl, mix flours, baking powder, and salt.
2. In other bowl, mix egg, milk, and shortening.
3. Pour milk mixture into dry ingredients and stir only enough to moisten dry ingredients. The mix should be lumpy. Too much beating makes the pancakes tough.
4. Add fruit, if used.
5. Pour from large mixing spoon onto hot, lightly greased griddle.
6. Flip and turn pancakes once.
7. Serve with maple syrup, wild jams, or jellies.

ACORN BREAD

Oven: 350°F   *Time: 20–30 minutes*

Ingredients   *Utensils*

  1 cup acorn flour   2 mixing bowls
  ½ cup cornmeal   Measuring cup
  ½ cup whole wheat flour   Measuring
  1 teaspoon salt   spoons
  1 tablespoon baking   Mixing spoon
     powder   Greased bread
  3 tablespoons cooking   pan or 8″ x 8″
     oil   cake pan
  1 egg
  ½ cup honey
  1 cup milk

Directions

1. Combine acorn flour, cornmeal, whole wheat flour, salt, and baking powder.
2. Combine egg, oil, honey, and milk.
3. Add to dry ingredients, mixing a bit at a time.
4. Pour into greased pan.
5. Bake at 350°F for 20 to 30 minutes or until toothpick inserted comes out clean.

ARROWHEAD

SCIENTIFIC NAME: *Sagittaria latifolia*

AUGUST–NOVEMBER

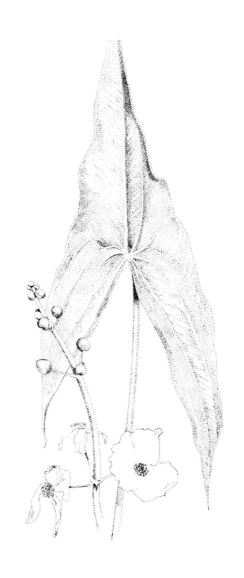

This shapely plant of pond and river margins is well named; each leaf has the form of an arrowhead. In summer three silky white flowers bloom atop an erect flower stalk. The fruits are round balls; within are the flat seeds. A distinctive feature of the arrowhead is the leaf veins that run from bottom to top like barrel slats.

Late in autumn the arrowheads produce, at the end of long slender roots, hard potatolike tubers about the size of a chicken egg, called a swamp or duck potato. These were once a staple for the American Indian the nation across.

The tubers are several feet away from the stems of the parent plant and usually a foot down. They form in midsummer but are most abundant in the autumn. The Indian squaws collected them by wading barefoot in the mud, feeling for the potatoes, and breaking them loose with their toes. They pop to the surface, for they are light and buoyant. A rake or a shovel can also be used.

The potatoes are slightly bitter when eaten raw. Boiled or baked in a rock oven, however, they are transformed into a delicious potato treat. The cooked tubers can be sliced, strung on strings Indian fashion, and dried for winter use.

Wear old clothes and foot gear when you go arrowhead tuber foraging—the plants love deep mire.

ARROWHEAD SALAD

Ingredients
- 1 package lemon gelatin
- 1 cup boiling water
- 1 teaspoon vinegar
- 1 tablespoon grated onion
- ¼ teaspoon salt
- 1 cup sour cream
- ¼ cup mayonnaise
- 1 cup finely chopped arrowhead tuber, fresh or cooked
- Black walnuts

Utensils
- 1-quart saucepan
- Measuring cup
- Measuring spoons
- Mixing spoon
- 1-quart circular mold with hole in the middle

Directions
1. Dissolve gelatin in boiling water.
2. Add vinegar, onion, and salt.
3. Let stand until syrupy.
4. Add sour cream and arrowhead.
5. Stir.
6. Pour into a mold and chill.
7. Top with black walnuts.

ARROWHEAD SOUP

Ingredients

4 leeks, sliced, or 1
   onion, sliced
¼ cup sweet butter
8 or 9 arrowhead tubers,
   cooked and sliced
   thinly
1 quart chicken bouillon
   or broth
1 tablespoon or less salt
3 cups milk
2 cups heavy cream
   Chopped wild garlic or
   chives

Utensils

4-quart saucepan
Measuring cup
Measuring
  spoons
Mixing spoon
Electric blender,
  or potato
  masher
Chopping board
Sharp knife

Directions

1. In a saucepan, brown the leeks in the butter.
2. Add the cooked arrowhead tubers, broth, and salt, and boil 5 minutes.
3. Mash tubers with potato masher, or put in electric blender to purée.
4. Return to saucepan, and add milk and cream.
5. Bring to a boil and serve hot, garnished with chives or wild chopped garlic leaves.
6. Or chill thoroughly and serve cold with green garnish.

ARROWHEAD TUBER BREAD

Oven: 400°F, then 350°F.   *Time: 55 minutes*

Ingredients
1½ cups hot mashed
    arrowhead tubers
½ cup soft butter
⅓ cup sugar
½ teaspoon salt
1 cup scalded sweet
    cream
2 packages yeast
⅓ cup warm water
6 cups flour
⅓ cup raisins
⅓ cup chopped nuts

Utensils
Large mixing
    bowl
Small mixing
    bowl
Measuring cup
Measuring
    spoons
Mixing spoon
Buttered bowl for
    rising
Lightly floured
    tabletop
Two buttered
    bread pans
Dishtowel
Pastry brush

Directions
1. Melt butter in hot mashed arrowhead tubers, then add sugar and salt.
2. Add scalded sweet cream and let cool.
3. Dissolve yeast in warm water and add to arrowhead tuber mix.

4. Stir in 3 cups flour, then gradually blend in the rest.
5. Stir in raisins and nuts.
6. Turn dough onto lightly floured table.
7. Knead dough 100 times by pressing it with heel of hand, then turning it and pressing again.
8. Place in buttered bowl, cover with dish-towel, and let rise until doubled, or for about one hour.
9. Punch down and shape into 2 loaves and place in buttered loaf pans.
10. Cover and let rise ½ hour.
11. Brush with melted butter and bake at 400°F for 10 minutes. Reduce heat to 350°F and bake another 45 minutes.

BLACK WALNUT

SCIENTIFIC NAME: *Juglans nigra*

OCTOBER–DECEMBER

This aromatic tree with its scaly and furrowed bark is found in rich river bottomlands and fertile hillsides from Massachusetts west to Minnesota, Nebraska, Kansas, and eastern Oklahoma and southward to Florida and the San Antonio River Valley. One subspecies grows in California, another in Texas and Oklahoma. All have thirteen to twenty-three leaflets that make one leaf. Each leaflet is about three inches long and one inch wide, of bright yellow-green. The whole compound leaf is one to two feet long. The flowers are stout, upward-growing bells that are rusty brown. The fruit grow singly or in pairs, with a thick husk that is used for stains and dye. The nut is thick-walled and requires a hammer to break.

It grows in temperate North America and is valued for its dark beautiful wood, used in furniture and house interiors.

The husks will dry out if gathered green. The nuts are ripe when the husks are dark brown-black and knock off easily with hands or a hammer. Crack the nut with a hammer and pick out meats with nut picker—a good job for the evening around the fireside or a rainy day listening to music.

APACHE WALNUT CORN BREAD

Oven: 350°F   *Time: 1 hour*

Ingredients
- 6 ears of fresh corn
- 1 teaspoon salt
- ½ cup chopped black walnuts

Utensils
- Measuring cup
- Food blender
- Sharp knife
- Mixing bowl
- Mixing spoon
- Bread pan
- Also can be cooked in bucket with lid in campfire coals

Directions
1. Shuck corn. Save the tenderest husks.
2. Store husks in plastic bag to prevent drying out.
3. Cut kernels off corn with sharp knife.
4. Grind kernels in a blender or a food grinder.
5. Line a small metal bread pan with the husks, reserving some husks for the top.
6. Combine the ground corn, salt, and walnuts.
7. Pour mixture on top of corn husks.

8. Cover with remaining husks.
9. Bake at 350°F for about an hour.
10. Check bread often to prevent overcooking. Should be springy and moist. An excellent recipe for a rock oven.

Also use black walnuts in Maple Syrup Black Walnut Cake (see page 62) and in cookies and cakes and on top of ice cream.

WALNUT AND/OR PECAN PIE

Ingredients

½ cup butter

¾ cup light brown sugar

3 eggs

1 cup light corn syrup

1 cup broken walnuts
   and/or pecans

1 teaspoon vanilla
   Pinch of salt

9" unbaked pie shell

Utensils

Mixing bowl

Measuring cup

Measuring
   spoons

Mixing spoon

Cookie sheet

Directions

1. Cream butter and light brown sugar.
2. Beat in eggs, one at a time.
3. Stir in corn syrup.
4. Stir in nuts.
5. Add vanilla and salt.
6. Pour into unbaked pie shell.
7. Place on cookie sheet.
8. Bake in preheated oven for 45 minutes.

CURRANTS
AND GOOSEBERRIES
SCIENTIFIC NAME: *Ribes* (VARIOUS SPECIES)
JUNE–SEPTEMBER

Currants and gooseberries are members of the rose family **Ribes**. *About fifteen species grow across the country; they are easily identified by the thorny stems and, in most species, a bristly fruit. The leaves are three- to five-lobed and resemble a maple leaf.*

Both currants and gooseberries are ball-shaped and often are marked with lines of bristles running from pole to pole. The bristly black currant is found in low woods and bogs, the common gooseberry in open woods, usually in and around pine forests in both the East and West. All species are enjoyed by rabbits, songbirds, grouse, bobwhites, skunks, foxes, and coyotes. I have never failed to run into some wild creature while gathering wild currants and gooseberries. Sit quietly for a while and you'll see them, too.

GOOSEBERRY PIE

Oven: 375°F   *Time: 1 hour*

Ingredients   *Utensils*
  1 9" pie crust   2 mixing bowls
  1 cup gooseberries   Measuring cup
  1 cup sugar   Measuring
¼ cup flour   spoons
  2 eggs   Eggbeater
  2 tablespoons water   Mixing spoon

Directions

1. Mix flour and sugar.
2. Beat egg and water slightly and add mixture to flour and sugar.
3. Wash gooseberries, drain, pick off stems.
4. Add berries to flour, sugar, egg, and water mix.
5. Place in crust and bake.
6. Serve with vanilla ice cream.

GRASS SEEDS

AUGUST–OCTOBER

All grass seeds can be eaten. Three of the best are dropseed, Sporobolus cryptandrus, *and panic grass,* Panicum ontusum *and P.* capillars, *largely because these are abundant and their seeds are the easiest to thrash out.*

Panic grass plants are mainly inhabitants of fields and upland waste places, but a few, such as maidencane and switch grass, are found in moist low areas.

If you can't identify the grass, any wild grass with seed heads will do just fine.

Because grass seeds are small and take time to gather and thrash, American Indians usually combine them with other flours to make bread or breakfast cereal.

Take an old cloth bag such as a pillowcase, or make one by sewing up a sheet. Put grass stems and seeds into the bag head first, and close. Bang heads lightly on the floor, or shake. The seeds and chaff will fall to the bottom. To remove chaff, either blow it away or pour it into a pan of water. The seeds sink, the chaff and hulls float and can be skimmed off.

Add to Dandelion Fritters, Acorn Bread, Sunflower Bread.

Grasses are vital to ground-feeding birds, small mammals, wild turkey, and many songbirds.

JERUSALEM ARTICHOKE

SCIENTIFIC NAME: *Helianthus tuberosus*

OCTOBER (AFTER KILLING FROST)–APRIL

This sunflower blooms in late August and September and bears a two- to three-inch flower. It is a tall plant, growing six to ten feet high, with rough leaves, the lower ones often opposite. The stems are hairy.

The Jerusalem artichoke sunflower prefers moist soil in the open, along fence rows or near ditches and streams, and grows all over the United States. Seeds can be bought from catalogues and grown in the yard as a constant and delicious food source. The tubers need not be dug up and stored for winter like potatoes. Rather, leave them in the ground and dig when needed. Be sure that a killing frost has touched the plants. The tubers are sweetest at this time. They are limp and less tasty after the plant begins to grow in April.

These succulent tubers are not only good eaten raw or cooked and mashed, but are excellent baked.

To be certain you have a Jerusalem artichoke, dig down to the roots of the sunflower plant. If the roots have tubers, you have hit gold. Some plants will yield as many as twenty tubers. The plant is neither an artichoke, as named, nor is it any way related to Jerusalem. The Biblical name is a mispronunciation of the Indian words for sun-follower.

MASHED JERUSALEM ARTICHOKES

Ingredients
- 12 to 15 Jerusalem artichoke tubers
- 1½ quarts water
- ¼ cup milk
- Butter
- Salt

Utensils
- Stiff brush
- Peeler
- Small knife
- Measuring cup
- 3-quart saucepan
- Colander
- Potato masher

Directions
1. Scrub tubers with a stiff brush, peel like a potato, and slice or quarter.
2. Bring water to a boil, add tubers.
3. Simmer for 25 minutes.
4. Drain off water.
5. Mash with milk, butter, and salt.
6. Serve hot.

(Also see Fiddlehead Pie, page 11; add raw to Weedy Lawn Salad, page 34.)

PINYON PINE

SCIENTIFIC NAME: *Pinus edulis,*
ALSO *Pinus monophylla* AND *Pinus cembroides*

This handsome tree, said to be the oldest food of the Pueblo Indians, has a short trunk and conic crown. The bark of old trees is grayish brown. The tree does not grow to the stature of other pines. The needles grow two or, rarely, three in a bundle.

The seeds supply a rich source of protein and fat, a pound containing 3,000 calories. The nuts can be preserved by shelling and baking in a 200°F oven for two hours, or preserved raw in the refrigerator for about six months.

The nuts are delicious as is or over fish, in salads, in pancakes and muffins. Add them to biscuit mix and fruit rolls. I like them best in pesto sauce.

PINYON NUT PESTO

Ingredients	*Utinsils*
Water	4-quart pot
4 tablespoons butter	Small saucepan
4 cups fresh basil	Measuring cup
1 or 2 cloves garlic,	Measuring
wild or domestic,	spoons
mashed or chopped	Garlic masher

Ingredients (*cont.*)
¼ cup pinyon nuts
½ cup Parmesan cheese
   Salt
½ cup olive oil
½ pound thin spaghetti

Utensils (*cont.*)
Food chopper or
   blender
Colander

Directions
1. Fill pot with water and bring to a boil.
2. While water is coming to a boil, soften butter in small saucepan.
3. Place basil, garlic, pinyon nuts, and cheese in blender.
4. To boiling water, add salt and 1 tablespoon of the olive oil.
5. Add sphagetti. Cook about 9 minutes for al dente. Drain. Put in large serving bowl.
6. Add rest of the olive oil and the softened butter to ingredients in blender.
7. Blend until a mush.
8. Pour over spaghetti.
9. Serve hot.

SQUAWBERRY
OR STAGHORN SUMAC

SCIENTIFIC NAMES: *Rhus trilobata* (WEST)

Rhus typhina (EAST)

AUGUST–OCTOBER

The squawberry is called staghorn sumac in the East and is a shrub with very hairy twigs. The leaves are made up of eleven to thirty-one toothed leaflets one or two feet long. They leave tooth-shaped leaf scars when broken off at the stem. The bark is brown and smooth, with numerous raised cross streaks. The leaf of the squawberry or western sumac has three oval leaflets, somewhat like oak leaves.

The fruit of the staghorn sumac is upright in clusters of dark red furry balls about a quarter of an inch around. The squawberry fruit, also red and about a quarter-inch long, are clustered close to the stems and covered with hairs. Both are somewhat sticky on the outside when fresh, and not particularly juicy. Both fruits taste lemony.

The berries can be boiled for a beverage or dried in a low oven, 200°F, for a winter tea.

STEWED
SUMAC OR SQUAWBERRIES

Ingredients

  3 cups dried or fresh
    squawberries
  4 tablespoons flour
2½ cups boiling water
  ⅓ cup sugar

Utensils

Food chopper or
  blender
Measuring cup
Measuring spoon
Mixing spoon
3-quart saucepan

Directions

1. Grind berries in blender, or chop.
2. Add flour.
3. Put berries in boiling water and stir.
4. Add sugar and serve.

HOT SQUAWBERRY TEA

Directions

1. Put a handful of squawberries into a pot of water while out hiking or camping and boil like tea.
2. Let stand for a while before drinking.
   or
1. Put 3 cups of fresh berries in a 2-quart jar.
2. Add 4 cups of water.
3. Let stand overnight.
4. Strain off juice.
5. Serve with ice and sugar to taste.

SQUAWBERRY BREAD

Oven: 400°F   *Time: 20–30 minutes*

Ingredients   *Utensils*
- 1 cup squawberries   Measuring cup
- 2 cups water   Mixing bowl
- ¼ cup sugar   Large mixing
- 1 cup biscuit mix   spoon
- ½ cup water   3-quart saucepan
- Butter or margarine   Food press
                        9″ bread or cake
                          pan

Directions

1. Mash squawberries and put into water (seeds will sink).
2. Bring to a boil, cover, and simmer for 15 to 20 minutes.
3. Pour off liquid and pulp. Discard seeds.
4. Squeeze pulp through food press.
5. Add ¼ cup sugar.
6. Mix biscuit mix and water until soft dough forms.
7. Fold squawberry pulp into dough.
8. Place in bread or cake pan or, if outdoors, camp bucket.
9. Bake until top is lightly browned.
10. Serve hot, with butter or margarine.

SUNFLOWER SEEDS

SCIENTIFIC NAME: *Helianthus annuus*

SEPTEMBER–NOVEMBER

(GATHER SEEDS FOR STORAGE OVER WINTER)

The sunflower is a common roadside native plant that grows throughout the Midwest and West. It is tall, with rough stout stems and coarse-toothed leaves. The large flower heads have showy yellow petals and yellow-brown or purple-brown centers. Stalks are three to seven feet high.

Sunflower seed meats can be extracted by spinning them in a food chopper and putting the crushed seeds in a bowl of water. The meats sink, the chaff floats.

A small plot of land exposed to sun in city or country can be sowed to sunflowers, which will yield many of these attractive flowers and their tasty seeds. Buy commercial seeds. They produce larger plants and more seeds.

SUNFLOWER PUDDING

Ingredients	Utensils (cont.)
1 cup corn kernels cut from fresh and very young corn (can be field corn)	Cutting board
	Knife
	Measuring cup
	Food grinder

Ingredients (cont.)

1 cup finely ground raw
   or roasted sunflower
   seeds (shelled)
1 cup finely chopped
   squash, zucchini, or
   yellow crookneck squash
2 cups water
1 teaspoon salt
   Butter
   Green chiles or green
   peppers, chopped

Utensils (cont.)

Measuring
   spoons
3-quart saucepan

Directions

1. Put corn kernels and sunflower seeds through food grinder.
2. Combine in a saucepan with squash, water, and salt.
3. Cover pot and simmer for 1 hour, stirring occasionally.
4. Remove lid toward end of cooking time to let mixture thicken.
5. Serve with butter and chopped green chiles or green peppers.

SUNFLOWER BREAD

Oven: 325°F   *Time: 1 hour*

Ingredients

¼ cup honey

¼ cup soft butter

2 eggs, beaten

1 cup whole wheat flour

1 tablespoon baking powder

1 teaspoon salt

1½ cups blender-ground sunflower seeds, meats only

1 cup milk

½ cup whole sunflower meats

Utensils

Blender

2 mixing bowls

Measuring cup

Measuring spoons

9″ greased bread pan

Directions

1. Cream together honey and butter.
2. Beat in eggs.
3. Combine flour, baking powder, salt, and ground seeds.
4. Add honey and butter mixture by alternately stirring into dry ingredients with milk.
5. Fold in whole sunflower seeds.
6. Put in greased bread loaf pan.
7. Bake 1 hour.
8. Cool on rack and slice.

WILD ROSE

SCIENTIFIC NAME: *Rosa arizonica* (WEST);
Rosa palustris, Rosa acicularis (EAST TO MIDWEST)
AUGUST–OCTOBER

More than thirty-five species of wild rose grow over the United States. They look like a typical garden rosebush with leaves having five or seven leaflets and thorny stems. The flowers have five large petals. The fruits, called rose hips, are usually bright red when ripe. Rose petals are excellent served in salads or sugared. Rose hips can be eaten raw, dried for tea, or cooked into jam, jelly, or syrup. The hips are rich in vitamin C and iron. To dry rose hips, place them on a cookie sheet in a 200°F. oven until crisp, and store in an airtight jar. The rose hips of domestic garden species are also edible and nutritious.

ROSE HIP JAM

Gather rose hips, wash, and snip the bud ends off with scissors.

Ingredients	*Utensils*
Water	Scissors
Rose hips	Kitchen scale
½ pound sugar for each	Measuring cup
pound of pulp	5-quart saucepan
Cinnamon	Sieve or food
	press

Utensils (cont.)
Large spoon
5 or 6 jelly jars
12-quart pot for
   boiling jars
Paraffin
Small pan in
   water in large
   pan
   for melting
   paraffin

Directions
1. Weigh the rose hips. Use 1 cup of water for each pound of rose hips.
2. Place rose hips and water in saucepan and simmer for 20 minutes.
3. Push the cooked pulp through a sieve or food press.
4. Weigh pulp, and add ½ pound of sugar for each pound of pulp.
5. Add a dash of cinnamon.
6. Simmer this mixture until it is thick and 2 drops run together on spoon, or use pectin and boil 2 minutes.
7. Pour into sterilized jars.
8. Cover jam with a thin layer of paraffin, cool, and store.

ALL YEAR 'ROUND

SABAL PALMETTO

SCIENTIFIC NAME: *Sabal palmetto*

ALL YEAR

The sabal palmettoes rise over the glades of southern Florida like round lollypops. The leaves, which are five to six feet long, and six to eight feet broad, resemble huge fans. Flowers grow on slender spikes, and the fruits, which ripen late in the autumn, are a bright chestnut color. The trees often reach forty to fifty feet in height; some are as tall as ninety feet. The trunk can be two feet in diameter.

They grow in the sandy soil from Cape Hatteras, Virginia, to the tip of Florida, but are most abundant along Florida's West Coast.

The people of Dade and Collier counties in Florida call these handsome trees "swamp cabbage trees" and "cabbage palms" because of their taste.

The whole tree must be cut down to get at the "cabbage," which is the bud or heart of the tree from which the leaves spring. It is several feet down in the trunk and has to be cut out with an ax or machete. One tree yields a cabbage about four inches in diameter and six to eight inches long.

BOILED HEART OF SABAL PALMETTO

Ingredients
Water
Salt
½ pound fatback
1 heart of a sabal palmetto

Utensils
4-quart pot

Directions
1. Bring salted water to a boil.
2. Put heart of palm and fatback in water.
3. Boil for 20 to 25 minutes. Do not overcook; it gets mushy.

My Florida friend who grew up on these treats says swamp cabbage *has* to be eaten with cornbread.

SASSAFRAS

SCIENTIFIC NAME: *Sassafras albidum*

ALL YEAR

The leaves of this tree are its distinguishing feature: the sassafras has three differently shaped leaves. One is an oval, another is three-lobed, and the third is shaped like a mitten. All parts of the tree are aromatic, so break the leaves, sniff, and taste for positive identification.

The bark on young trees is reddish-brown. Old trunks are dark red-brown and divided into broad flat ridges with deep grooves between.

The tree grows from southern Maine to the middle of Florida and west Texas to Michigan, and attains immense proportions along the east coast. It is often found in old fields and forest openings.

SASSAFRAS TEA

Directions

1. With a shovel dig down about 4 feet from a large sassafras tree until you find roots.
2. Smell or taste them to confirm the fact that you have sassafras.
3. Cut them off with garden shears or ax.

4. Wash and cut off the bark with a penknife or with a vegetable peeler. The bark is the essence of the tea.
5. Discard inner wood.
6. Lay bark out to dry in a well-ventilated place, or put on cookie sheet and heat in 200°F oven for 3 or 4 hours.

Ingredients	*Utensils*
4 cups water	Pot
3 to 5 inch-long strips of sassafras root bark	Strainer
Cream	
Sugar	

Directions
1. Put root bark in pot with water.
2. Bring to a boil and simmer for 10 or 15 minutes.
3. Strain and serve. (Keep root bark for reuse 3 or 4 times.)
4. Add cream and sugar if desired.

This is one of the great treats of the wilds. The Seneca Indians used the concentrated oil as a laxative and to lower fevers.

WISHAKAPUCKA
OR LABRADOR TEA
SCIENTIFIC NAME: *Ledum groenlandicum*
ALL YEAR

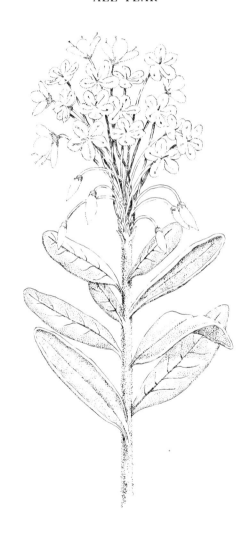

A shrub about three feet high, with woody stems covered with reddish hairs. The untoothed leaves, which are alternate, leathery, and evergreen, are oval and very dark green on the upper side. The undersides have a white or rusty wool. The leaf edges roll over the wooly underside, making the plant quite distinctive. The white flowers are bunched at the end of stems, and the fruit is slender and egg-shaped. The plant is fragrant and tastes snappy and clean.

When John Franklin, the polar explorer from 1819 to 1823, ran out of food on one occasion, he wrote, "We drank an infusion of the Labrador tea plant and ate a few morsels of burnt leather for supper." The Indians call the plant Wishakapucka, a rollicking name for this excellent rhubarblike tea.

LABRADOR TEA

Ingredients
1 pot of boiling water
1 cup leaves, stems, fruit,
   and flowers of Labrador
   tea plant
Sugar
Cream

Utensils
Tea strainer
Pot

Directions
1. Boil plant parts for 15 minutes.
2. Let stand 3 minutes.
3. Strain off tea into cups.
4. Add sugar and cream, or drink as is.

INDEX